Adventure to Ava's School

• Respecting Authority •

By T. M. Merk

Published by The Child's World®
1980 Lookout Drive • Mankato, MN 56003-1705
800-599-READ • www.childsworld.com

Photographs: wavebreakmedia/Shutterstock.com, cover, 1, 7, 9,
15, 17, 19; Velazquez77/Shutterstock.com, 4; Lorelyn Medina/
Shutterstock.com, 11; SeventyFour/Shutterstock.com, 13
Icons: © Aridha Prassetya/Dreamstime, 3, 5, 9, 10, 13, 22

ISBN HARDCOVER: 9781503827431
ISBN PAPERBACK: 9781622434381
LCCN: 2017961929

Printed in the United States of America
PA02379

About the Author

T.M. Merk is an elementary educator
with a master's degree in elementary
education from Lesley University in
Cambridge, Massachusetts. Drawing
on years of classroom experience, she
enjoys creating engaging educational
material that inspires students' passion
for learning. She lives in New Hampshire
with her husband and her dog, Finn.

Table of Contents

Adventure to Ava's School

It was time for art class. Ava loved art class!

"Today we will learn about warm and cool colors," said her art teacher, Mrs. Conners.

What does **authority** mean? Authority is a person (or people) who is in charge or has control. Teachers are the authority in the classroom because they are the leaders of the students in their room. Police officers are the authority in your town because they help to make sure everyone follows the laws. The president is the authority for the United States of America because he or she is the leader of our government.

"I know," Ava **interrupted**. "The warm colors are red, yellow, orange, pink, and brown. The cool colors are blue, green, purple, and gray."

"Good, Ava, but next time, please raise your hand. Remember, we all agreed that it is a classroom rule," replied Mrs. Conners.

"Why?" whined Ava.

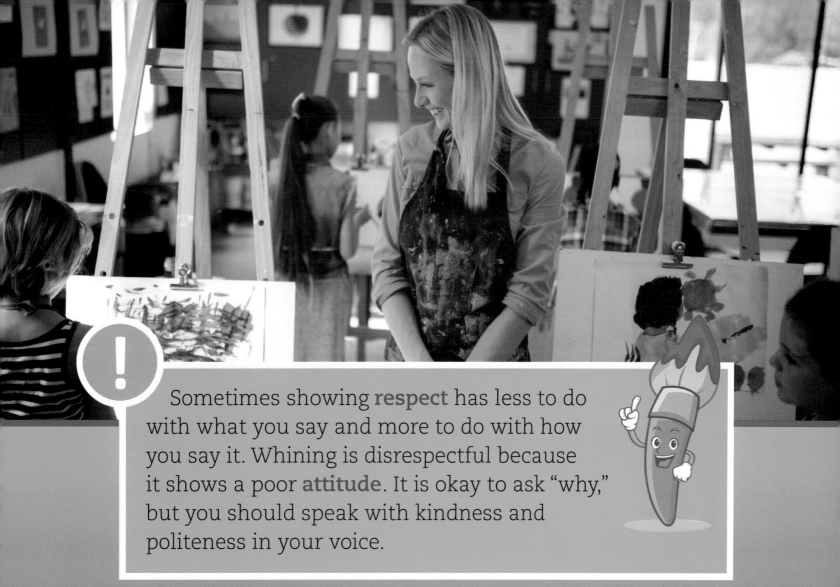

Sometimes showing **respect** has less to do with what you say and more to do with how you say it. Whining is disrespectful because it shows a poor **attitude**. It is okay to ask "why," but you should speak with kindness and politeness in your voice.

9

Leo the paintbrush shook at Ava's work space.

"Ava, **disregard** for classroom rules is not respectful," he said. "It's time to brush up on respect."

Following the rules is one way to show respect to the classroom authority, your teacher. Your teacher works hard to create a place where everyone can learn. The rules help to teach you what it means to be respectful, such as being polite and listening. Following classroom rules is respectful to your teacher and his or her classroom.

Classroom Rules

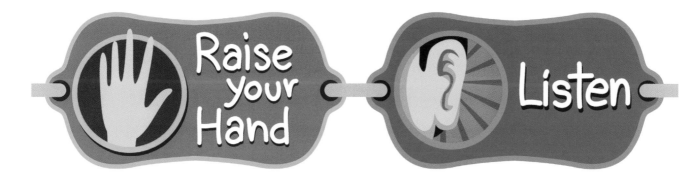

Raise your Hand

Listen

Be a friend

Help Clean Up

"Hi, Leo. Does 'respectful' mean following rules?" Ava asked.

Leo nodded. "That is part of being respectful. Your class made a **promise** to follow the rules. It is respectful to raise your hand before you speak or leave your seat. You promised to listen, share, and keep your work space clean."

Many students work together with their teacher at the beginning of the school year to create a classroom **contract**. This means that the students and the teacher make rules that they think would help to create a respectful classroom for the year.

"I don't understand those rules," Ava said. "Why do I need to stay in my seat all of the time?"

"Your teacher wants you to pay attention and learn," Leo explained.

15

"Even when I know the answer?" Ava asked.

"Yes," Leo said. "When you interrupt someone, that person feels bad. It seems like you don't care about what he or she says. Mrs. Conners might feel like you don't respect her."

17

"That would be awful," Ava moaned. "Mrs. Conners teaches us a lot! Now I see how the rules we made help us learn together."

19

Respectful Talk

Do you need help talking in a respectful way to people in authority? Use these sentence starters to help!

- May I please ... ?

- Is now a good time for ... ?

- Do you mind if I ... ?

- After this, could we ... ?

- I liked it when you said ...

- Could you please explain ... ?

- Would you please help me with ... ?

S.T.E.A.M. Activity

Create a Gift for an Adult You Respect in Your School

Directions: Using any materials that you choose, create a gift for an adult you respect in your school. What does he or she like? It is thoughtful and respectful to create something that you know another person cares about.

Time Constraints: You may use a total of 30 minutes for your creation. You are allowed 10 minutes to plan and 20 minutes to create your gift. When you're done, surprise your chosen person with the special gift.

Discussion: Did you take time to think about what the person cares about? Did you ever become frustrated when making this project? If you did, how did you help yourself have a good attitude? What worked really well? What could you do better next time?

Suggested Materials:

- Construction paper
- Clay
- Beads
- Pipe cleaners
- Tape
- Glue
- Safety scissors
- Markers/crayons

Glossary

attitude: (AT-tih-tood) Your attitude is how you feel about someone or something.

authority: (uh-THOR-ih-tee) Authority is a person (or people) who is in charge or has control.

contract: (KON-trakt) A contract is a written or verbal agreement.

disregard: (dis-reh-GARD) To disregard is to ignore.

interrupt: (in-ter-RUPT) To interrupt is to talk when someone else is talking.

promise: (PRAH-miss) A promise is an agreement to do or not do something.

respect: (rih-SPEKT) To respect is to show that you care about a person, place, thing, or idea.

To Learn More

Books

Cook, Julia. *My Mouth is a Volcano.* Chattanooga, TN: National Center for Youth Issues, 2006.

Javernick, Ellen. *What if Everybody Did That?* Tarrytown, NY: Marshall Cavendish Pinwheel Books, 2010.

Rankin, Laura. *Ruthie and the (Not So) Teeny Tiny Lie.* New York, NY: Bloomsbury U.S.A. Children's Books, 2007.

Web Sites

Visit our Web site for links about respecting people in authority:
childsworld.com/links

Note to Parents, Teachers, and Librarians: We routinely verify our Web links to make sure they are safe and active sites. So encourage your readers to check them out!

Index